Personal Internet Log Of

LOGIN INFORMATION

WEBSITE:

USERNAME:

PASSWORD:

SECURITY QUESTIONS

UPDATES:

***

WEBSITE:

USERNAME:

PASSWORD:

SECURITY QUESTIONS

UPDATES:

LOGIN INFORMATION

WEBSITE:

USERNAME:

PASSWORD:

SECURITY QUESTIONS

UPDATES:

***

WEBSITE:

USERNAME:

PASSWORD:

SECURITY QUESTIONS

UPDATES:

LOGIN INFORMATION

A

WEBSITE:

USERNAME:

PASSWORD:

SECURITY QUESTIONS

UPDATES:

***

WEBSITE:

USERNAME:

PASSWORD:

SECURITY QUESTIONS

UPDATES:

LOGIN INFORMATION

WEBSITE:

USERNAME:

PASSWORD:

SECURITY QUESTIONS

UPDATES:

***

WEBSITE:

USERNAME:

PASSWORD:

SECURITY QUESTIONS

UPDATES:

LOGIN INFORMATION

WEBSITE:

USERNAME:

PASSWORD:

SECURITY QUESTIONS

UPDATES:

***

WEBSITE:

USERNAME:

PASSWORD:

SECURITY QUESTIONS

UPDATES:

LOGIN INFORMATION

WEBSITE:

USERNAME:

PASSWORD:

SECURITY QUESTIONS

UPDATES:

***

WEBSITE:

USERNAME:

PASSWORD:

SECURITY QUESTIONS

UPDATES:

LOGIN INFORMATION

WEBSITE:

USERNAME:

PASSWORD:

SECURITY QUESTIONS

UPDATES:

***

WEBSITE:

USERNAME:

PASSWORD:

SECURITY QUESTIONS

UPDATES:

LOGIN INFORMATION

WEBSITE:

USERNAME:

PASSWORD:

SECURITY QUESTIONS

UPDATES:

***

WEBSITE:

USERNAME:

PASSWORD:

SECURITY QUESTIONS

UPDATES:

LOGIN INFORMATION

WEBSITE:

USERNAME:

PASSWORD:

SECURITY QUESTIONS

UPDATES:

***

WEBSITE:

USERNAME:

PASSWORD:

SECURITY QUESTIONS

UPDATES:

LOGIN INFORMATION

WEBSITE:

USERNAME:

PASSWORD:

SECURITY QUESTIONS

UPDATES:

✱✱✱

WEBSITE:

USERNAME:

PASSWORD:

SECURITY QUESTIONS

UPDATES:

LOGIN INFORMATION

WEBSITE:

USERNAME:

PASSWORD:

SECURITY QUESTIONS

UPDATES:

***

WEBSITE:

USERNAME:

PASSWORD:

SECURITY QUESTIONS

UPDATES:

LOGIN INFORMATION

WEBSITE:

USERNAME:

PASSWORD:

SECURITY QUESTIONS

UPDATES:

*** ***

WEBSITE:

USERNAME:

PASSWORD:

SECURITY QUESTIONS

UPDATES:

LOGIN INFORMATION

WEBSITE:

USERNAME:

PASSWORD:

SECURITY QUESTIONS

UPDATES:

***

WEBSITE:

USERNAME:

PASSWORD:

SECURITY QUESTIONS

UPDATES:

LOGIN INFORMATION

WEBSITE:

USERNAME:

PASSWORD:

SECURITY QUESTIONS

UPDATES:

$$***$$

WEBSITE:

USERNAME:

PASSWORD:

SECURITY QUESTIONS

UPDATES:

LOGIN INFORMATION

WEBSITE:

USERNAME:

PASSWORD:

SECURITY QUESTIONS

UPDATES:

***

WEBSITE:

USERNAME:

PASSWORD:

SECURITY QUESTIONS

UPDATES:

LOGIN INFORMATION

WEBSITE:

USERNAME:

PASSWORD:

SECURITY QUESTIONS

UPDATES:

***

WEBSITE:

USERNAME:

PASSWORD:

SECURITY QUESTIONS

UPDATES:

LOGIN INFORMATION

WEBSITE:

USERNAME:

PASSWORD:

SECURITY QUESTIONS

UPDATES:

✱✱✱

WEBSITE:

USERNAME:

PASSWORD:

SECURITY QUESTIONS

UPDATES:

LOGIN INFORMATION

WEBSITE:

USERNAME:

PASSWORD:

SECURITY QUESTIONS

UPDATES:

***

WEBSITE:

USERNAME:

PASSWORD:

SECURITY QUESTIONS

UPDATES:

LOGIN INFORMATION

WEBSITE:

USERNAME:

PASSWORD:

SECURITY QUESTIONS

UPDATES:

***

WEBSITE:

USERNAME:

PASSWORD:

SECURITY QUESTIONS

UPDATES:

LOGIN INFORMATION

WEBSITE:

USERNAME:

PASSWORD:

SECURITY QUESTIONS

UPDATES:

$$***$$

WEBSITE:

USERNAME:

PASSWORD:

SECURITY QUESTIONS

UPDATES:

LOGIN INFORMATION

WEBSITE:

USERNAME:

PASSWORD:

SECURITY QUESTIONS

UPDATES:

***

WEBSITE:

USERNAME:

PASSWORD:

SECURITY QUESTIONS

UPDATES:

LOGIN INFORMATION

WEBSITE:

USERNAME:

PASSWORD:

SECURITY QUESTIONS

UPDATES:

***

WEBSITE:

USERNAME:

PASSWORD:

SECURITY QUESTIONS

UPDATES:

LOGIN INFORMATION

WEBSITE:

USERNAME:

PASSWORD:

SECURITY QUESTIONS

UPDATES:

***

WEBSITE:

USERNAME:

PASSWORD:

SECURITY QUESTIONS

UPDATES:

LOGIN INFORMATION

WEBSITE:

USERNAME:

PASSWORD:

SECURITY QUESTIONS

UPDATES:

***

WEBSITE:

USERNAME:

PASSWORD:

SECURITY QUESTIONS

UPDATES:

LOGIN INFORMATION

WEBSITE:

USERNAME:

PASSWORD:

SECURITY QUESTIONS

UPDATES:

***

WEBSITE:

USERNAME:

PASSWORD:

SECURITY QUESTIONS

UPDATES:

LOGIN INFORMATION

WEBSITE:

USERNAME:

PASSWORD:

SECURITY QUESTIONS

UPDATES:

***

WEBSITE:

USERNAME:

PASSWORD:

SECURITY QUESTIONS

UPDATES:

G LOGIN INFORMATION

WEBSITE:

USERNAME:

PASSWORD:

SECURITY QUESTIONS

UPDATES:

***

WEBSITE:

USERNAME:

PASSWORD:

SECURITY QUESTIONS

UPDATES:

LOGIN INFORMATION

WEBSITE:

USERNAME:

PASSWORD:

SECURITY QUESTIONS

UPDATES:

***

WEBSITE:

USERNAME:

PASSWORD:

SECURITY QUESTIONS

UPDATES:

LOGIN INFORMATION

WEBSITE:

USERNAME:

PASSWORD:

SECURITY QUESTIONS

UPDATES:

***

WEBSITE:

USERNAME:

PASSWORD:

SECURITY QUESTIONS

UPDATES:

LOGIN INFORMATION

WEBSITE:

USERNAME:

PASSWORD:

SECURITY QUESTIONS

UPDATES:

***

WEBSITE:

USERNAME:

PASSWORD:

SECURITY QUESTIONS

UPDATES:

LOGIN INFORMATION

WEBSITE:

USERNAME:

PASSWORD:

SECURITY QUESTIONS

UPDATES:

***

WEBSITE:

USERNAME:

PASSWORD:

SECURITY QUESTIONS

UPDATES:

LOGIN INFORMATION

WEBSITE:

USERNAME:

PASSWORD:

SECURITY QUESTIONS

UPDATES:

***

WEBSITE:

USERNAME:

PASSWORD:

SECURITY QUESTIONS

UPDATES:

LOGIN INFORMATION

WEBSITE:

USERNAME:

PASSWORD:

SECURITY QUESTIONS

UPDATES:

***

WEBSITE:

USERNAME:

PASSWORD:

SECURITY QUESTIONS

UPDATES:

LOGIN INFORMATION

WEBSITE:

USERNAME:

PASSWORD:

SECURITY QUESTIONS

UPDATES:

***

WEBSITE:

USERNAME:

PASSWORD:

SECURITY QUESTIONS

UPDATES:

I LOGIN INFORMATION

WEBSITE:

USERNAME:

PASSWORD:

SECURITY QUESTIONS

UPDATES:

***

WEBSITE:

USERNAME:

PASSWORD:

SECURITY QUESTIONS

UPDATES:

LOGIN INFORMATION

WEBSITE:

USERNAME:

PASSWORD:

SECURITY QUESTIONS

UPDATES:

***

WEBSITE:

USERNAME:

PASSWORD:

SECURITY QUESTIONS

UPDATES:

J LOGIN INFORMATION

WEBSITE:

USERNAME:

PASSWORD:

SECURITY QUESTIONS

UPDATES:

***

WEBSITE:

USERNAME:

PASSWORD:

SECURITY QUESTIONS

UPDATES:

LOGIN INFORMATION

WEBSITE:

USERNAME:

PASSWORD:

SECURITY QUESTIONS

UPDATES:

***

WEBSITE:

USERNAME:

PASSWORD:

SECURITY QUESTIONS

UPDATES:

LOGIN INFORMATION

J

WEBSITE:

USERNAME:

PASSWORD:

SECURITY QUESTIONS

UPDATES:

***

WEBSITE:

USERNAME:

PASSWORD:

SECURITY QUESTIONS

UPDATES:

LOGIN INFORMATION

J

WEBSITE:

USERNAME:

PASSWORD:

SECURITY QUESTIONS

UPDATES:

***

WEBSITE:

USERNAME:

PASSWORD:

SECURITY QUESTIONS

UPDATES:

LOGIN INFORMATION

WEBSITE:

USERNAME:

PASSWORD:

SECURITY QUESTIONS

UPDATES:

$$***$$

WEBSITE:

USERNAME:

PASSWORD:

SECURITY QUESTIONS

UPDATES:

LOGIN INFORMATION

WEBSITE:

USERNAME:

PASSWORD:

SECURITY QUESTIONS

UPDATES:

***

WEBSITE:

USERNAME:

PASSWORD:

SECURITY QUESTIONS

UPDATES:

LOGIN INFORMATION

WEBSITE:

USERNAME:

PASSWORD:

SECURITY QUESTIONS

UPDATES:

***

WEBSITE:

USERNAME:

PASSWORD:

SECURITY QUESTIONS

UPDATES:

LOGIN INFORMATION

WEBSITE:

USERNAME:

PASSWORD:

SECURITY QUESTIONS

UPDATES:

***

WEBSITE:

USERNAME:

PASSWORD:

SECURITY QUESTIONS

UPDATES:

LOGIN INFORMATION

WEBSITE:

USERNAME:

PASSWORD:

SECURITY QUESTIONS

UPDATES:

***

WEBSITE:

USERNAME:

PASSWORD:

SECURITY QUESTIONS

UPDATES:

LOGIN INFORMATION

WEBSITE:

USERNAME:

PASSWORD:

SECURITY QUESTIONS

UPDATES:

***

WEBSITE:

USERNAME:

PASSWORD:

SECURITY QUESTIONS

UPDATES:

LOGIN INFORMATION

WEBSITE:

USERNAME:

PASSWORD:

SECURITY QUESTIONS

UPDATES:

***

WEBSITE:

USERNAME:

PASSWORD:

SECURITY QUESTIONS

UPDATES:

LOGIN INFORMATION

WEBSITE:

USERNAME:

PASSWORD:

SECURITY QUESTIONS

UPDATES:

***

WEBSITE:

USERNAME:

PASSWORD:

SECURITY QUESTIONS

UPDATES:

LOGIN INFORMATION

WEBSITE:

USERNAME:

PASSWORD:

SECURITY QUESTIONS

UPDATES:

***

WEBSITE:

USERNAME:

PASSWORD:

SECURITY QUESTIONS

UPDATES:

LOGIN INFORMATION

WEBSITE:

USERNAME:

PASSWORD:

SECURITY QUESTIONS

UPDATES:

***

WEBSITE:

USERNAME:

PASSWORD:

SECURITY QUESTIONS

UPDATES:

LOGIN INFORMATION

WEBSITE:

USERNAME:

PASSWORD:

SECURITY QUESTIONS

UPDATES:

***

WEBSITE:

USERNAME:

PASSWORD:

SECURITY QUESTIONS

UPDATES:

LOGIN INFORMATION

WEBSITE:

USERNAME:

PASSWORD:

SECURITY QUESTIONS

UPDATES:

***

WEBSITE:

USERNAME:

PASSWORD:

SECURITY QUESTIONS

UPDATES:

LOGIN INFORMATION

N

WEBSITE:

USERNAME:

PASSWORD:

SECURITY QUESTIONS

UPDATES:

***

WEBSITE:

USERNAME:

PASSWORD:

SECURITY QUESTIONS

UPDATES:

LOGIN INFORMATION

WEBSITE:

USERNAME:

PASSWORD:

SECURITY QUESTIONS

UPDATES:

***

WEBSITE:

USERNAME:

PASSWORD:

SECURITY QUESTIONS

UPDATES:

N **LOGIN INFORMATION**

WEBSITE:

USERNAME:

PASSWORD:

SECURITY QUESTIONS

UPDATES:

$$***$$

WEBSITE:

USERNAME:

PASSWORD:

SECURITY QUESTIONS

UPDATES:

LOGIN INFORMATION

WEBSITE:

USERNAME:

PASSWORD:

SECURITY QUESTIONS

UPDATES:

***

WEBSITE:

USERNAME:

PASSWORD:

SECURITY QUESTIONS

UPDATES:

LOGIN INFORMATION

WEBSITE:

USERNAME:

PASSWORD:

SECURITY QUESTIONS

UPDATES:

***

WEBSITE:

USERNAME:

PASSWORD:

SECURITY QUESTIONS

UPDATES:

LOGIN INFORMATION

WEBSITE:

USERNAME:

PASSWORD:

SECURITY QUESTIONS

UPDATES:

***

WEBSITE:

USERNAME:

PASSWORD:

SECURITY QUESTIONS

UPDATES:

LOGIN INFORMATION

WEBSITE:

USERNAME:

PASSWORD:

SECURITY QUESTIONS

UPDATES:

***

WEBSITE:

USERNAME:

PASSWORD:

SECURITY QUESTIONS

UPDATES:

LOGIN INFORMATION

WEBSITE:

USERNAME:

PASSWORD:

SECURITY QUESTIONS

UPDATES:

***

WEBSITE:

USERNAME:

PASSWORD:

SECURITY QUESTIONS

UPDATES:

LOGIN INFORMATION

WEBSITE:

USERNAME:

PASSWORD:

SECURITY QUESTIONS

UPDATES:

***

WEBSITE:

USERNAME:

PASSWORD:

SECURITY QUESTIONS

UPDATES:

LOGIN INFORMATION

WEBSITE:

USERNAME:

PASSWORD:

SECURITY QUESTIONS

UPDATES:

*** ***

WEBSITE:

USERNAME:

PASSWORD:

SECURITY QUESTIONS

UPDATES:

LOGIN INFORMATION

WEBSITE:

USERNAME:

PASSWORD:

SECURITY QUESTIONS

UPDATES:

***

WEBSITE:

USERNAME:

PASSWORD:

SECURITY QUESTIONS

UPDATES:

LOGIN INFORMATION

WEBSITE:

USERNAME:

PASSWORD:

SECURITY QUESTIONS

UPDATES:

***

WEBSITE:

USERNAME:

PASSWORD:

SECURITY QUESTIONS

UPDATES:

Q **LOGIN INFORMATION**

WEBSITE:

USERNAME:

PASSWORD:

SECURITY QUESTIONS

UPDATES:

$$***$$

WEBSITE:

USERNAME:

PASSWORD:

SECURITY QUESTIONS

UPDATES:

LOGIN INFORMATION

WEBSITE:

USERNAME:

PASSWORD:

SECURITY QUESTIONS

UPDATES:

***

WEBSITE:

USERNAME:

PASSWORD:

SECURITY QUESTIONS

UPDATES:

LOGIN INFORMATION

WEBSITE:

USERNAME:

PASSWORD:

SECURITY QUESTIONS

UPDATES:

***

WEBSITE:

USERNAME:

PASSWORD:

SECURITY QUESTIONS

UPDATES:

LOGIN INFORMATION

WEBSITE:

USERNAME:

PASSWORD:

SECURITY QUESTIONS

UPDATES:

***

WEBSITE:

USERNAME:

PASSWORD:

SECURITY QUESTIONS

UPDATES:

LOGIN INFORMATION

WEBSITE:

USERNAME:

PASSWORD:

SECURITY QUESTIONS

UPDATES:

***

WEBSITE:

USERNAME:

PASSWORD:

SECURITY QUESTIONS

UPDATES:

LOGIN INFORMATION

WEBSITE:

USERNAME:

PASSWORD:

SECURITY QUESTIONS

UPDATES:

***

WEBSITE:

USERNAME:

PASSWORD:

SECURITY QUESTIONS

UPDATES:

LOGIN INFORMATION

WEBSITE:

USERNAME:

PASSWORD:

SECURITY QUESTIONS

UPDATES:

***

WEBSITE:

USERNAME:

PASSWORD:

SECURITY QUESTIONS

UPDATES:

LOGIN INFORMATION

WEBSITE:

USERNAME:

PASSWORD:

SECURITY QUESTIONS

UPDATES:

***

WEBSITE:

USERNAME:

PASSWORD:

SECURITY QUESTIONS

UPDATES:

S **LOGIN INFORMATION**

WEBSITE:

USERNAME:

PASSWORD:

SECURITY QUESTIONS

UPDATES:

***

WEBSITE:

USERNAME:

PASSWORD:

SECURITY QUESTIONS

UPDATES:

LOGIN INFORMATION

WEBSITE:

USERNAME:

PASSWORD:

SECURITY QUESTIONS

UPDATES:

***

WEBSITE:

USERNAME:

PASSWORD:

SECURITY QUESTIONS

UPDATES:

S   LOGIN INFORMATION

WEBSITE:

USERNAME:

PASSWORD:

SECURITY QUESTIONS

_____

_____

_____

UPDATES:

$$***$$

WEBSITE:

USERNAME:

PASSWORD:

SECURITY QUESTIONS

_____

_____

_____

UPDATES:

LOGIN INFORMATION

WEBSITE:

USERNAME:

PASSWORD:

SECURITY QUESTIONS

UPDATES:

*** *** ***

WEBSITE:

USERNAME:

PASSWORD:

SECURITY QUESTIONS

UPDATES:

LOGIN INFORMATION

T

WEBSITE:

USERNAME:

PASSWORD:

SECURITY QUESTIONS

_____

_____

_____

UPDATES:

***

WEBSITE:

USERNAME:

PASSWORD:

SECURITY QUESTIONS

_____

_____

_____

UPDATES:

LOGIN INFORMATION

T

WEBSITE:

USERNAME:

PASSWORD:

SECURITY QUESTIONS

UPDATES:

***

WEBSITE:

USERNAME:

PASSWORD:

SECURITY QUESTIONS

UPDATES:

LOGIN INFORMATION

T

WEBSITE: _____

USERNAME: _____

PASSWORD: _____

SECURITY QUESTIONS

_____

_____

_____

UPDATES: _____

***

WEBSITE: _____

USERNAME: _____

PASSWORD: _____

SECURITY QUESTIONS

_____

_____

_____

UPDATES: _____

LOGIN INFORMATION

WEBSITE:

USERNAME:

PASSWORD:

SECURITY QUESTIONS

UPDATES:

***

WEBSITE:

USERNAME:

PASSWORD:

SECURITY QUESTIONS

UPDATES:

LOGIN INFORMATION

WEBSITE:

USERNAME:

PASSWORD:

SECURITY QUESTIONS

WEBSITE:

***

UPDATES:

USERNAME:

PASSWORD:

SECURITY QUESTIONS

UPDATES:

LOGIN INFORMATION

WEBSITE:

USERNAME:

PASSWORD:

SECURITY QUESTIONS

UPDATES:

***

WEBSITE:

USERNAME:

PASSWORD:

SECURITY QUESTIONS

UPDATES:

LOGIN INFORMATION

WEBSITE:

USERNAME:

PASSWORD:

SECURITY QUESTIONS

UPDATES:

***

WEBSITE:

USERNAME:

PASSWORD:

SECURITY QUESTIONS

UPDATES:

LOGIN INFORMATION

WEBSITE:

USERNAME:

PASSWORD:

SECURITY QUESTIONS

UPDATES:

***

WEBSITE:

USERNAME:

PASSWORD:

SECURITY QUESTIONS

UPDATES:

LOGIN INFORMATION

WEBSITE:

USERNAME:

PASSWORD:

SECURITY QUESTIONS

UPDATES:

***

WEBSITE:

USERNAME:

PASSWORD:

SECURITY QUESTIONS

UPDATES:

LOGIN INFORMATION

WEBSITE:

USERNAME:

PASSWORD:

SECURITY QUESTIONS

UPDATES:

***

WEBSITE:

USERNAME:

PASSWORD:

SECURITY QUESTIONS

UPDATES:

LOGIN INFORMATION

WEBSITE:

USERNAME:

PASSWORD:

SECURITY QUESTIONS

UPDATES:

***

WEBSITE:

USERNAME:

PASSWORD:

SECURITY QUESTIONS

UPDATES:

LOGIN INFORMATION

WEBSITE:

USERNAME:

PASSWORD:

SECURITY QUESTIONS

UPDATES:

***

WEBSITE:

USERNAME:

PASSWORD:

SECURITY QUESTIONS

UPDATES:

LOGIN INFORMATION

WEBSITE:

USERNAME:

PASSWORD:

SECURITY QUESTIONS

UPDATES:

***

WEBSITE:

USERNAME:

PASSWORD:

SECURITY QUESTIONS

UPDATES:

LOGIN INFORMATION

WEBSITE:

USERNAME:

PASSWORD:

SECURITY QUESTIONS

UPDATES:

$$***$$

WEBSITE:

USERNAME:

PASSWORD:

SECURITY QUESTIONS

UPDATES:

LOGIN INFORMATION

WEBSITE:

USERNAME:

PASSWORD:

SECURITY QUESTIONS

UPDATES:

***

WEBSITE:

USERNAME:

PASSWORD:

SECURITY QUESTIONS

UPDATES:

LOGIN INFORMATION

WEBSITE:

USERNAME:

PASSWORD:

SECURITY QUESTIONS

UPDATES:

***

WEBSITE:

USERNAME:

PASSWORD:

SECURITY QUESTIONS

UPDATES:

LOGIN INFORMATION

WEBSITE:

USERNAME:

PASSWORD:

SECURITY QUESTIONS

UPDATES:

***

WEBSITE:

USERNAME:

PASSWORD:

SECURITY QUESTIONS

UPDATES:

LOGIN INFORMATION

WEBSITE:

USERNAME:

PASSWORD:

SECURITY QUESTIONS

UPDATES:

***

WEBSITE:

USERNAME:

PASSWORD:

SECURITY QUESTIONS

UPDATES:

LOGIN INFORMATION

WEBSITE:

USERNAME:

PASSWORD:

SECURITY QUESTIONS

UPDATES:

***

WEBSITE:

USERNAME:

PASSWORD:

SECURITY QUESTIONS

UPDATES:

LOGIN INFORMATION

WEBSITE:

USERNAME:

PASSWORD:

SECURITY QUESTIONS

UPDATES:

***

WEBSITE:

USERNAME:

PASSWORD:

SECURITY QUESTIONS

UPDATES:

LOGIN INFORMATION

WEBSITE:

USERNAME:

PASSWORD:

SECURITY QUESTIONS

UPDATES:

***

WEBSITE:

USERNAME:

PASSWORD:

SECURITY QUESTIONS

UPDATES:

LOGIN INFORMATION

WEBSITE:

USERNAME:

PASSWORD:

SECURITY QUESTIONS

UPDATES:

***

WEBSITE:

USERNAME:

PASSWORD:

SECURITY QUESTIONS

UPDATES:

LOGIN INFORMATION

WEBSITE:

USERNAME:

PASSWORD:

SECURITY QUESTIONS

UPDATES:

***

WEBSITE:

USERNAME:

PASSWORD:

SECURITY QUESTIONS

UPDATES:

LOGIN INFORMATION

WEBSITE:

USERNAME:

PASSWORD:

SECURITY QUESTIONS

UPDATES:

***

WEBSITE:

USERNAME:

PASSWORD:

SECURITY QUESTIONS

UPDATES:

Z LOGIN INFORMATION

WEBSITE:

USERNAME:

PASSWORD:

SECURITY QUESTIONS

UPDATES:

***

WEBSITE:

USERNAME:

PASSWORD:

SECURITY QUESTIONS

UPDATES:

LOGIN INFORMATION

Z

WEBSITE:

USERNAME:

PASSWORD:

SECURITY QUESTIONS

UPDATES:

***

WEBSITE:

USERNAME:

PASSWORD:

SECURITY QUESTIONS

UPDATES:

LOGIN INFORMATION

Z

WEBSITE:

USERNAME:

PASSWORD:

SECURITY QUESTIONS

UPDATES:

✳✳✳

WEBSITE:

USERNAME:

PASSWORD:

SECURITY QUESTIONS

UPDATES:

LOGIN INFORMATION

Z

WEBSITE:

USERNAME:

PASSWORD:

SECURITY QUESTIONS

UPDATES:

***

WEBSITE:

USERNAME:

PASSWORD:

SECURITY QUESTIONS

UPDATES:

FAVORITE WEBSITE ADDRESSES

FAVORITE WEBSITE ADDRESSES

NOTES

NOTES

Find more organizational books at
amazon.com/author/lindyknowles

Flamingo Press
PUBLISHING